To Nathan, for believing I could —C. A.

To my sister, my mom, and all of
the strong women in my life —T. B.

Henry Holt and Company, *Publishers since 1866*
Henry Holt® is a registered trademark of Macmillan Publishing Group, LLC
120 Broadway, New York, NY 10271 • mackids.com

Library of Congress Cataloging-in-Publication Data
Names: Andros, Camille, author. | Blackham, Tessa, illustrator.
Title: From a small seed : the story of Eliza Hamilton / Camille Andros ; illustrated by Tessa Blackham.
Other titles: Story of Eliza Hamilton
Description: First edition. | New York : Henry Holt and Company, [2019] | "Christy Ottaviano Books."
    Includes bibliographical references. | Audience: Ages 4–9.
Identifiers: LCCN 2019003102 | ISBN 9781250297426 (hardcover)
Subjects: LCSH: Hamilton, Elizabeth Schuyler, 1757–1854—Juvenile literature. | Hamilton, Alexander, 1757–1804—
    Family—Juvenile literature. | Politicians' spouses—United States—Biography—Juvenile literature.
Classification: LCC E302.6.H22 A53 2019 | DDC 973.4092 [B] —dc23
LC record available at https://lccn.loc.gov/2019003102

Our books may be purchased in bulk for promotional, educational, or business use. Please contact your local bookseller or the
Macmillan Corporate and Premium Sales Department at (800) 221-7945 ext. 5442 or by email at MacmillanSpecialMarkets@macmillan.com.

First edition, 2019 / Design by Mallory Grigg
The artist created the art in this book with gouache, colored pencil, and digital rendering.
Printed in China by Toppan Leefung Printing Ltd., Dongguan City, Guangdong Province
10 9 8 7 6 5 4 3 2 1

FROM A
SMALL SEED

the story of
Eliza Hamilton

Camille Andros

illustrated by
Tessa Blackham

Christy Ottaviano Books

Henry Holt and Company
New York

Eliza grew up in a big brick house
surrounded by a grove of tall, tall trees
with branches strong for swinging.
The trees started as small seeds.
The small seeds grew into saplings.
Saplings with shallow roots
blew over when storms came.

But the trees whose roots
reached down deep
survived and became strong.

When she was a child,
Eliza's parents tucked her covers in tight,
kissed her scraped knees,
and softly sang her lullabies.

As a girl, Eliza climbed hills,

hopped fences,

and impressed leaders.

Her dark eyes were bright
and brilliant with promise.

Like the saplings, she was young and green.

But her mind was sharp, her faith was strong,

and her heart was light.

Every day Eliza saw the same
little boy as she rode by.
An orphan.
A child with no parents.

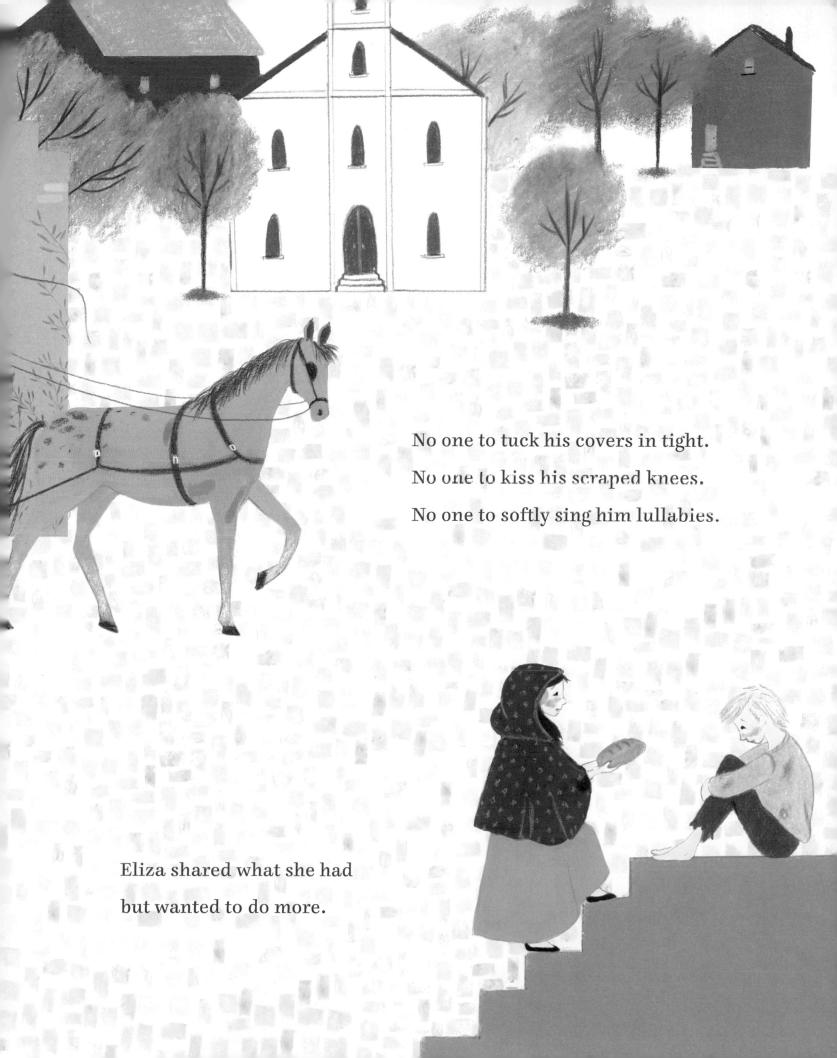

No one to tuck his covers in tight.

No one to kiss his scraped knees.

No one to softly sing him lullabies.

Eliza shared what she had
but wanted to do more.

Then the boy was gone.

The stoop was empty.

And the carriage rolled on.

But Eliza did not forget.

Time passed.

Eliza grew like the trees she used to swing from.

She blossomed like flowers on branches in spring.

One day, she met another orphan.
In his eyes Eliza saw brightness,
brilliance, and promise.
His mind was sharp, his faith was
strong, and he gave his heart to Eliza.
Eliza loved the young man and
married him.

They believed in fairness, freedom, and faith.

Passion, persistence, and perseverance.

They helped found a new nation.

Together they had eight children,
and with Eliza's sharp mind,
strong faith, and kind heart,
she planted seeds.

She taught them fairness, freedom, and faith.
He taught them passion, persistence, and perseverance.
A new generation of saplings started to grow.

But tragedy hit the
Hamilton household.

Life—like the wind—can be harsh.
A weaker tree would have fallen, yet
Eliza's roots were deep.

Then, once again, Eliza met a little boy

who was an orphan.

In his eyes Eliza saw the same

brightness, brilliance, and promise

she had seen before in another orphan boy long ago.

Eliza had not forgotten.

And now she knew what to do.

She planted thousands of seeds when she started the
Orphan Asylum Society and the Hamilton Free School.
She taught fairness, freedom, and faith.
Passion, persistence, and perseverance.

Eliza was planting a forest.

With each child she loved,

she grew.

Her roots were deep.

Her branches wide.

She was strong.

For another fifty years Eliza still climbed hills,

hopped fences,

and impressed leaders.

She raised money for refugees,
opened her home to the homeless,
gave bundles of food and clothing
to those in need.

She remembered.

But after ninety-seven years,
it was time for Eliza to rest.

So she did.
In a quiet place
surrounded by a grove of tall, tall trees
with branches strong for swinging.

Eliza's story isn't one that the world much noticed until recently. While I have fictionalized the part of the story where young Eliza sees the orphan boy as she drives by, her traits of empathy and compassion were likely part of her character. Eliza carried herself with an unassuming, quiet grace. Because few of her letters exist today, we have limited firsthand information about her, but a careful study of her life shows an enduring strength of character that speaks for itself.

Elizabeth Schuyler Hamilton, or Eliza as she was often called, was born on August 9, 1757, in Albany, New York, the second daughter of Catherine van Rensselaer Schuyler and Philip Schuyler. Her father was a former military officer and businessman, and her mother came from one of the wealthiest families in New York. Eliza grew up wanting for nothing, with seven brothers and sisters to play with and keep her company. Short and athletic, she clambered up hills with ease when others needed help. Eliza's good nature and bright eyes left a lasting impression.

At thirteen, she went with her father to a meeting of chiefs of the Six Nations in Saratoga, New York, where she received an American Indian name meaning "one of us." Benjamin Franklin taught her how to play backgammon when he visited her father in 1776.

Eliza first met Alexander Hamilton in 1777 when she was twenty years old. He had come to visit her father, by then a Revolutionary War general, on business for General George Washington. She met him again in February 1780, and their relationship flourished. They were engaged in April and married that December.

Eliza assisted Alexander as he worked with others to found a new nation. "He made your government," Eliza told a young man in 1853. "He made your bank. I sat up all night with him to help him do it . . . I sat up all night, copied out his writing, and the next morning, he carried it to President Washington and we had a bank."

She was good friends with Martha Washington, who was always Eliza's "ideal of a true woman."

Mrs. Washington once left a pair of pink satin slippers at Eliza's father's house that became one of Eliza's few surviving personal items.

In the summer of 1797, when Eliza was pregnant with her sixth child, a string of tragedies began to unravel. First, a scandal involving her husband was publicly exposed. Then in 1801 her oldest son, Philip, was killed in a duel. Eliza's older daughter, Angelica, suffered a mental breakdown after Philip's death and was never the same. Eliza's mother and her sister Margarita (Peggy) died during that time as well. Then in 1804 her husband was shot and killed in a duel. Four months later her father died.

That Eliza went on to serve and help others after all the tragedy she had experienced shows the strength, compassion, and empathy of an extraordinary woman. In 1806, less than two years after the death of Alexander, she cofounded the New York Orphan Asylum Society, and in 1818 she started the Hamilton Free School, the first educational institution in the Washington Heights section of Manhattan.

She was sharp, spry, and quick-witted even in her old age. In her eighties, instead of taking a carriage from the train station to her son's home, she would cut across meadows and hop two fences as a shortcut. When she was ninety-one years old, she moved to Washington, D.C., to live with her widowed daughter. She helped her friend Dolley Madison raise money for the Washington Monument. Eliza had a nearly constant stream of distinguished visitors, senators, and even presidents who came to pay their respects to one of the last connections to Revolutionary days.

Eliza outlived her husband by fifty years, raised seven children, and dedicated her life to preserving her husband's good name and caring for the orphaned and less fortunate. She is an unsung heroine and a founding mother of our country, whose stoic strength stands as a lasting legacy of faith, wisdom, grace, and compassion.

Artist's Note

Although Elizabeth Schuyler Hamilton is one of our nation's founding mothers, the information about her life is not as complete as one would hope. This made the illustrative research challenging, though my visit to Eliza's childhood home in Albany, New York, was helpful and inspiring. There I discovered the blue damask wallpaper in the children's room, the distant Cohoes Falls that Eliza climbed hills to see, and the golden gage plum tree her father cultivated.

I did take a few creative liberties to better illustrate Eliza's story. For instance, Eliza met Benjamin Franklin when she was eighteen years old, but I elected to illustrate her as a young girl to better chronicle the evolution of her childhood years. And while Abraham Lincoln lived during Eliza's time, there is no evidence that Eliza actually met him. I believe, based on his admiration of George Washington, a close friend and colleague to Alexander, that Lincoln would have been delighted to meet Eliza.

My special thanks to the members of the Schuyler Mansion State Historic Site for answering my questions and endeavoring to keep Eliza's story alive.

Bibliography

Chernow, Ron. *Alexander Hamilton*. New York: Penguin Group, 2004.

Graham Windham. "A Rich History of Over 212 Years," accessed November 20, 2018, Graham-Windham.org.

Miranda, Lin-Manuel, and Jeremy McCarter. *Hamilton the Revolution*. New York: Hachette, 2016.